EDWARD ELGAR

Give unto the Lord
Opus 74

for SATB and Organ or Orchestra

Psalm xxix

Edited by Bruce Wood

NOVELLO

Published in Great Britain by Novello Publishing Limited
(a division of The Music Sales Group)
14/15 Berners Street, London W1T 3LJ

Exclusive distributors: Music Sales Limited, Newmarket Road
Bury St Edmunds, Suffolk, IP33 3YB
tel: +44 (0)1284 702600   fax: +44 (0)1284 702592
Order No. NOV320056
www.chesternovello.com

Preface

Elgar began work on *Give unto the Lord* on 7 February 1914. He evidently worked very fast, for by 24 March the vocal score was already in print; but, even though the work had been conceived with orchestral accompaniment, he did not undertake the task of scoring it until 9-11 April, only three weeks before the first performance, which was given at the Festival of the Sons of the Clergy in St. Paul's Cathedral on 30 April. The printed vocal score is in general agreement with the autograph (London, British Library, Add. MS 58034, ff. 41-72), only a few small details of the organ part and of the divisions in the soprano and alto parts having been adjusted during proof-correction.

When orchestrating the piece, however, Elgar changed a good many details of the accompaniment, some of them merely phrasing or articulation marks, but others affecting the notes themselves. In consequence, some passages in the published full score (the whereabouts of the autograph are unknown) are not accurately represented by the organ part in the published vocal score. This new edition of the latter brings the two into agreement; besides emendations involving only the markings, there are more substantial changes in bars 30, 54-57, 71, 73, 82, 111, 127 and 133.

Both the vocal and the orchestral score are full of Elgar's characteristic markings of phrasing, articulation and expression, and of his highly specific directions as to flexibility of pulse, which he carefully distinguished from the main tempo indications. He was aware that some performers, especially singers, found his score markings unduly restrictive. "Would you give yourself the trouble", he once wrote to W.G. McNaught of Novello, "to look over a proof [of some part-songs] with an eye – two eyes – to expression-marks and stage directions? I overdo this sort of thing (necessary in orchestral stuff) as I put down all my feelings as I write and then haven't the heart to take 'em out." For the attentive performer, nonetheless, Elgar's markings are as important as the notes themselves.

I am grateful to the Librarians and authorities of the British Library for their unfailing helpfulness, and for permission to consult materials among their holdings in the preparation of this new edition.

BRUCE WOOD
School of Music
University of Wales, Bangor
Summer 2004

GIVE UNTO THE LORD

EDWARD ELGAR, Op.74
Edited by Bruce Wood

Psalm xxix